HowExpert Presents

Trucking Business Secrets

How to Start, Run, and Grow Your Trucking Company

HowExpert with Bruce Stimson

For more tips related to this topic, visit
HowExpert.com/truckingbusiness.

Recommended Resources

- HowExpert.com – Quick 'How To' Guides on All Topics from A to Z by Everyday Experts.
- HowExpert.com/free – Free HowExpert Email Newsletter.
- HowExpert.com/books – HowExpert Books
- HowExpert.com/courses – HowExpert Courses
- HowExpert.com/clothing – HowExpert Clothing
- HowExpert.com/membership – HowExpert Membership Site
- HowExpert.com/affiliates – HowExpert Affiliate Program
- HowExpert.com/writers – Write About Your #1 Passion/Knowledge/Expertise & Become a HowExpert Author.
- HowExpert.com/resources – Additional HowExpert Recommended Resources
- YouTube.com/HowExpert – Subscribe to HowExpert YouTube.
- Instagram.com/HowExpert – Follow HowExpert on Instagram.
- Facebook.com/HowExpert – Follow HowExpert on Facebook.

Table of Contents

Chapter 1: Define the Role of the Broker and Agent

Are you stuck in a dead end job and looking for a way out? Perhaps you have no job at all? Or maybe owning your own company is what you are most passionate about?

Well, you have come to the right place. While the freight and transportation business may not be for everyone, there's the possibility that this is the *gold mine* and *goal mind* you have been searching for.

Entrepreneur Magazine has rated the freight brokerage business as one of the top home-based businesses to own. A recent Wall Street Journal article cited freight brokering and logistics as the largest growing sector of the transportation industry. Let me tell you more about the ever growing industry of freight brokerage company and process agent career.

The transportation brokerage industry has experienced exponential growth over the past thirty years. Many shippers face the challenge of seeking opportunities to establish relationships with reliable freighters. It is the goal of both the shipper and carrier to work hard to get freight moved. Being able to solve the problem and get reliable and consistent transportation in the marketplace is the goal of all in the freight and transportation business.

Challenging issues faced by freighters include limitations of seasonal issues and specialized freight handling requirements. As a result, a number of challenges exist for both the carrier and shippers.

Advantages of Working Under a Brokerage Agency

Are there advantages to a position as a transportation broker or agent in the transportation industry? How about owning a brokerage company? Brokers are specialists who have expertise at moving freight in an efficient and professional manner, with rates negotiated on a load-by-load basis with the carrier.

The answer is an absolute yes.

While starting you own agency is financially beneficial, there are many benefits of working for a brokerage agency.

- The work that goes into a business startup can be tremendous and labor intensive.
- The trust confident business relationship between carriers, shippers and other brokerage firms in the logistic industry are close to impossible to establish for the new company that is just starting up.
- Other advantages include low overhead and startup cost of operating a freight brokerage agency. Below are a further examples of the benefits of working under a brokerage agency.
- The cost of liability insurance may not be a hindrance but the chances of a new company being able to secure a general liability policy may prove difficult or near impossible.
- It is important to have additional insurance coverage in case of loss or damage occurances that

the carrier's insurance does not cover. While the law does not require a company to hold a Contingent Cargo policy, it is highly recommended.

- Other costs and added expenses associated with the freight brokerage company that are not absorbed by an agent includes surety bond. The surety bond may not be expensive, but it is an additional expense.
- Another additional expense includes a marketing plan.
- The checks and balances (necessary in the transportation freight company) are a gateway to a successful business.
- The experience gained by working with an existing freight company can provide the internal workings necessary for a successful brokerage company. Take advantage of this eye opening experience and situate yourself in a position to "learn while you earn."
- A potential agent working under the leadership and training of a brokerage firm will not be responsible for any of the cost associated with the agency. It is the job of the agent to secure freight and cover the shipper's transportation needs.
- The firm supplies resources for all expenses with no charges to the agent.
- Most brokerage firms will offer an agent a lucrative percentage of the net profits or a smaller percentage of the growth revenue.
- In a typical situation, the agent is able to ask for an increased commission as the level of knowledge and experience increases.

Starting a brokerage allows you to profit by matching carriers with available capacity to shippers needs in the transportation services.

Chapter 2: Here's How the Industry Works

The primary goal is to have the broker help lower the transportation costs of the shipper while allowing the shipper to focus on its internal operations.

Got Freight Ready To Go? Here's How It Moves:

1. A contract for carriage, called a bill of lading, is issued by the carrier. The bill of lading is attached to each freight load and follows each load through the supply chain. The bill of lading describes the terms and condition of shipment. It tells who is responsible for the freight being shipped. While there may be other documents that accompany the negotiated process, the bill of lading represents the largest part of the carriage process. The bill of lading may be the only carriage contract and may function as the delivery receipt or document of title.
2. In some cases, the shipper contracts directly with a carrier or the shipper contracts with an intermediary, the broker. The broker is 'the middleman' who is responsible for matching cargo from a shipper, with a carrier in order to successfully complete the transportation requirement.
3. In some cases, a shipper has not negotiated a contractual relationship with a carrier and

cannot find an available carrier to haul its freight. The shipper may look to a broker for assistance.

4. The broker sends the freight bill to the shipper and pays the carrier.
5. Once the load is moved and the appropriate freight bills or invoices are sent and received, each party issues payment to the other to complete the transaction.

Where is the Bottom Line – The Profit?

The difference between what is billed to shipper and what is paid the carrier, serves as the broker's profit.

The broker must price its service high, to cover the freight bill amount owed to the carrier, but low enough to still remain competitive.

If the broker's price charged is too low, the broker will fail to make enough money on the transaction. If the broker's price charged is too high, then the broker fails to retain the much needed business to other brokers.

Effective execution of the process determines how large of a profit the broker will make. The broker must work to secure freight from the shippers that pay the broker more than what the broker will owe the carrier for executing carriage services.

If the shipper can obtain competitive rates from carriers and basically cover the load for the same rates offered through the broker, what else can compel the shipper to seek the services of other brokers?

You've got this!

Increase Your Business with Value-Added Service

The value-added service that a broker provides can encourage the supplier to use the services of the broker. Examples include:

1. Finding and dispatching carriers when the shipper does not have
    time to arrange for the shipment. Because the shipper does not have to arrange for the transportation services on its own, the shipper may decide to do business with the broker.
2. Tracking and tracing the load from origin to destination and making the information readily available to the shipper.
3. Consolidating billing to the shipper that allows the shipper to receive a summary bill that includes multiple shipments.

Carrier Benefits Too!

As a broker, a carrier may choose to work with your firm to acquire business he may not otherwise obtain.

The availability of back haul load for carriers may seem appealing and profitable on a return trip.

Please be advised there are risks involved in this business, as the same as risks involved in any business. To better understand your obligations and the obligation of all others - - you will need to attend the class.

Why Get Operating Authority

It is always good to have a reason to do things, and this applies to getting your operating authority. If you are considering getting your authority without a reason for doing so (a plan), you will have more difficulty than necessary. Yes, you can succeed because there is so much potential, but you would be behind the eight ball for a little while. With that said, I will just give a few common reasons as to why people prefer get their authority.

Financial

This is by far the most common reason as to why people get their authority. Someone hauling freight with their own authority can earn substantially more money than a company driver, lease purchase driver, or a leased owner. Whether it is for a freight forwarder (broker) or a shipper, the income will always be more.

Shipping Own Product

This is the second most common reason people have to get their authority. Many companies ,you may be familiar with them, have their own authority so they can save money on freight charges. Typically this would be a company that moves a lot of something on a continual basis. The best known big company that has their own authority is Walmart; they operate as a megacarrier.

More Home Time

The way most carriers force company drivers to stay on the road for extended periods of time is repulsive. There is no justification for a person to tell another person that they have to choose between spending time with their family or being employed. Being able to dictate your own schedule, while still having a good income, is a huge motivation. To be perfectly honest, I applaud people who use this as motivation to get their authority. It shows courage, responsibility, and devotion. My reason for getting our authority was twofold. First, my wife was diagnosed with breast cancer and I needed to be home for her more than a few days per month. Second, we needed to have good income to pay the bills. Getting our authority was absolutely the right choice because there was no way I could make ends meet the same way I did as a company driver and be home as much as I was.

Region and Customers

This is probably the shakiest reason for getting your authority, but it makes sense to some. Let's say that you are a company driver and your company usually designates you to drive in the northwest, during the winter, and then on the east coast during the summer. Or your company always has you at a shipper's dock at outrageous hours of the overnight, and they expect you to adjust your sleep schedule on a day's notice. Nobody will blame you for getting aggravated. Driving in the winter northwest over and over again is not good. It is not a matter of IF something bad happens; it is a matter of WHEN. Some crazy stuff happens there and I have seen enough craziness to write an entire book about. Driving on the east coast during the summer is simply a headache. The Baltimore, DC, Philly, NJ, NY, and Boston metropolitan chain is unbelievable at times. If your company continually sends you to a customer that takes several hours to load or unload trucks, that is very bad too. Using this as motivation to get your own authority, no one would fault you for it.

I will not go into too much detail in this chapter because it should be a pretty obvious concept to understand. Have at least a decent reason to get your authority.

When you embark on getting your own authority, you will need to have the following below completed:

1. You will need a source of freight. (Have all your potential customer contacts already lined up.

2. You will need to have a business identity and EIN (Employer Identification Number). You get this from the IRS (Internal Revenue Service). Type "Employer Identification Number" into Google. You will see at least one IRS website at the top of the results. Visit their site to set up your business. It is free. I have already informed you that you would need to know something about business at the beginning of this book. Here is where you will need to use that knowledge.
3. Have a reliable truck and trailer. (You will be shown how to get these later in the book)
4. Have your insurance provider lined up. Type "Commercial Vehicle Insurance" into Google.
5. Have your truck and trailer apportioned. (Have it registered in your home state with a license plate [Base Plate] from that state, as well as the registrations for all the other states you plan to operate your vehicle in). Your home state will apportion your vehicle in all the other states you wish to operate in. Call your state's Department Of Motor Vehicles (DMV) for directions of how to register a truck.
6. Have cost cutting on your mind AT ALL TIMES!
7. Have at least some method of accurately tracking all expenses and income. (Notice the order used: EXPENSES AND INCOME. Income is easy to track, but not knowing your expenses WILL put you out of business eventually)

You definitely want to have a good reason for everything you do in this industry. That philosophy will keep you out of trouble in all facets of life and in trucking. The trucking industry has the luxury of being able to recover from small miscues, but not many of them. Doing things without good reasoning will inevitably lead to miscues. Don't get in the habit of making miscues!

The Money in Trucking

This chapter will explain the money in trucking. Get out your calculator because you may need it to follow some of the examples. When you are a company driver, you don't have a chance to see these numbers. The motor carrier you drive for does see these numbers and makes business decisions every day because of them. When you get your authority, you will NEED to understand what this chapter explains.

When a truck moves a load of freight across the country, this is what happens.

1. Someone has decided to pay to ship that freight by truck

2. Someone has negotiated with that shipper for a rate (shipping price)

3. Someone produced a driver and truck to ship the freight

4. That driver and truck brings the freight to its destination

These four steps always happen when freight is shipped by truck. There are slight variations that will be explained now.

Contracted Freight

When you are a company driver for a major motor carrier, most of the loads you deliver will contract loads. This means that a particular shipper has signed a contract with a specific motor carrier. This shipper most likely has had many loads that need to be shipped. When this motor carrier and shipper got together to negotiate a rate to ship all these loads, the motor carrier gave the shipper a quantity discount and the shipper gave the motor carrier many loads. The motor carrier needed to have the capacity (drivers and trucks) to handle all that freight. It is not likely that you can get contracted freight when you get your own authority. You will also need to have Contract Carrier Authority which will be explained in Chapter 6.

Spot Freight

This is when a shipper has a small amount of loads (or simply one load) to ship. This shipper seeks to have this freight shipped "on the spot" which is where the term "spot freight" comes from. This is non-contracted freight. This freight typically pays the best. This shipper negotiates a rate to deliver a particular load. This shipper either negotiates a rate with a broker or directly with a motor carrier. When you become a motor carrier, you can obtain this type of freight. It is difficult to make all those cold calls to find shippers yourself, but it can definitely be done.

Freight Forwarding (Brokers)

This is the most abundant freight in the industry. The brokers have a system set up where they have access to an astounding amount of shippers shipping spot freight. This is why you most likely will deal with brokers when you get your authority. There are advantages and disadvantages to dealing with brokers. The advantages to dealing with brokers are:

1. They always have loads for you

2. The particulars of a load (Pickup #, pickup time, shipper information, delivery time) will be provided

3. The brokers know the rates for all lanes (routes) and typically get the most they can out of shippers

The disadvantages of dealing with brokers are:

1. They will always get a percentage of what that shipper pays to ship that freight

2. You will usually not be able to approach that shipper yourself to negotiate freight shipments for a specified period because of the agreement you sign before you do business with that particular broker

Cost of Doing Business

Knowing your costs is more important than anything else! You are most likely accustomed to some form of mileage based pay due to your experience as a company driver. That methodology is ok for analysis of income only. More pay per mile means better income right? You can also calculate your fuel cost per mile. There are other costs you will incur that do not translate to mileage based analysis at all. Your taxes are based upon income. Your insurance costs the same regardless of mileage. Permitting and licensing costs the same regardless of mileage. When you are a motor carrier, you will have the following costs.

1. Fuel

2. Insurance

3. Taxes (this is income tax, state and federal business fees, fuel tax, and highway use tax)

4. Bank Fees (this is monthly fees, interest charges, and transaction fees)

5. Driver Pay (this is what you pay yourself and drivers who work for you if you are able to grow your business that big. This will be your 2nd largest expense next to fuel)

6. Equipment Maintenance

7. Equipment Finance Payments

Chapter 3: Abide by the Industry's Standards

As in every industry, there will be things that will happen, things that will go wrong and the hard decisions that must be made. Some will affect the bottom line of your business, your driver and maybe even the customer. Usually in the transportation industry as in others, issues will arise out of someone's improper decision-making and incorrect application of key ethics in business.

While ethics and morals both relate to right and wrong, morals are established internally and ethics are external rules. Ethics are a series of beliefs that society arrives at, chosen and adopted individually by each person. Morals are a societal idea that a specific action is evil or immoral and another specific action is good or moral.

Being ethical and trustworthy in the logistics industry as in any other business is imperative. You will be dealing with customers, carriers, and other business associates and your word is all you have. Confidence and trust must be present in order for your business and you to become successful.

If your company has spent thousands of dollars building a brand and a reputation in the industry and your promise to provide a service at a determined cost, and you cannot – you are etching your way into a position of not being able to be trusted. Not only are you committing to a disservice to your company, you are also destroying a reputation. Clear up the problem as quickly as possible.

Here is a quick rule of success: Always be loyal to your company. When making decisions, you must always focus on one key issue – which decision is in the best interest of your company. Focus on what is advantageous financially, legally and operationally to your organization and what decision is best to achieve its goals.

In most businesses, we can agree that the primary focus is making a profit. However, if this is done at the expense of others and other companies, and if you conduct business with little or no regard for others, your industry-wide reputation in this service-providing industry will lead to a significant loss of business.

Means and ends refer to obtaining a result (end) and how you plan to achieve that outcome (means). While each of us acts a little differently in how we practice our personal "code of ethics," there are criterias for each organization in every industry that should remain intact by each of its agents. The criterias help to secure that a good and credible job will be done by all.

A reminder – in your day-to-day business dealings you will come across people, companies, drivers, repair centers, lumpers, carriers, and customers willing to take part in unethical behaviors. Donl come across people, companies, drivers, repair centers, lumpers, carriers, and ly in how we practice our personal "code of ethics," there are o enjoy a satisfying career in the transportation brokerage industry.

Even though the possibilities are unlimited, here are examples of some *unethical business practices* to look out for in your business efforts:

• Unethical Carriers' Behavior may try to falsify information such as insurance coverage limits, operating status, or other highly relevant information. They may "steal" or "back-solicit" the customer. Some carriers may hire drivers and not pay them. They may contract to pick up freight and leave you and your customer in a difficult problem if they choose to cancel without notification.

• Unethical Customers' Behavior may not pay the broker for services provided. They may arbitrarily deduct unforeseen revenue from the payment or book trucks not knowing for certain they will have freight to haul.

• Unethical Brokers' Behavior may book trucks without knowing for certain that they will have freight to haul.

• They may misrepresent the carrier's reputation to the customer, insurance coverage, or the carrier's legal authority to carry freight. They may not pay invoices, or pay invoices late, or attempt to underpay or deduct from legitimate charges. Brokers may contract to move freight then leave customers in a difficult position by cancelling without notification.

But, please don't be dismayed. We will cover methods, questions, and contracts to protect you from unethical practices. Remember morals and ethics are your reputation and your reputation is vital in achieving success with business.

If you work for a brokerage firm, you must keep its success in mind, and operate as such. That may mean passing on an opportunity that could be lucrative but presents ethical issues ahead. It should be the long-term interest of the company that becomes your top priority. By following the ruled of loyal and ethical behavior for your organization, you will help to ensure your career, your reputation, your company's brand and success as a whole.

You will be asked to make basic business decision every day in your dealing with the logistic trade. It is important to remember that these decisions will have a long-term effect on your business, your company and you, whether positive or negative.

Terms to consider and remember when making decisions

- Morals- societyo consider and remember whe
- *Ethics* thicsyo consider and remember when making *Autonomy* - the ability to freely determine oneking decisionsin life
- *Means and ends* eans and ends to freely determine oneking decisionsto get there.

If the load is delivered without incidents, you should pay the carrier, even if the shipper does not pay you. This is the foundation of ethical business relationships and will likely serve to benefit you and your company in the long run.

Remember, it is doing what you say you will do, regardless of its impact on immediate profitability. These are the true tests of ethics and morality.

Chapter 4: Satisfy the Steps to Become an Agent

We are looking for highly motivated individuals to grow with us. This terrific opportunity is open for aggressive Freight Agents to join us. We are proud of the relationship we have with each of our partners throughout the United States.

You don't need your own current customer or carrier base. All you need to have is a desire to learn the fright broker business in real time. We are looking for motivated, independent, people with good work ethics and strong entrepreneurial spirit to work with us as an independent freight agent.

As an agent, you will receive:

- An agreed upon minimum and maximum of the profit for all shipments with unlimited earnings potential.
- Use of the company insurance and bonds
- Use of the company brand name and online recognition
- Direct deposit payment of your commissions
- Technology needed for success
- An opportunity to partner with a logistics company as an independent full-time Contractor (1099).
- Do you have what it takes to run one of these businesses? Personality matters, but it is not something that cannot be learned. You may need some of the following traits:
  o Excellent Customer Services Qualities
  o Flexibility
  o Persistence and energy

- o Patience
- o Helpful experience

In additional to having personality, there is a range of skills and experience needed to run a business. When operating your business solo, you may need all of these characteristics to some degree.

As a general rule, you could benefit by having some kind of experience and understanding the concepts of sales and marketing. While you don't need a degree, it helps to be good at selling.

Determining Your Strengths

Take a list at the above list of character traits with yourself in mind. Which of these characteristics do you possess? Are you a take charge type person? Are you an organized whiz? How good are you at multitasking? What kind of experience do you have? What do you see as your major strengths and/or weaknesses?

Next think about the kind of lifestyle you prefer. You must be able to wear many hats. A transportation brokerage industry agent or broker's life may constitute:

- Long hours
- Completing many task at one time
- Communicating via telephone for many hours
- Constant interruptions
- Open lines of communications

- Open-minded
- Ability to follow through

With this position, you will be a 1099 independent freight agent and participate in efforts to grow and increase the market presence of your company as a premier freight transportation & logistic provider.

The main focus of the position is to build a solid client base of shippers and carriers. You will be in contact with client's daily, building relationships, solving problems, and assessing customer needs to make sure they are met along with the company's goals.

You will work with IT dispatch software and some other shipper database tools to help to locate and identify quality shippers and customers.

Chapter 5: Understand the Industry's Work Environment

Gone are the days when freight brokers used ledger books to track their loads. Most pertinent information about a load was kept in a ledger book. All shipments were entered in the ledger and each shipment was given a progressive number. Each load included the ship date, delivery date, invoice date, invoice amount, agreed rate with the carrier, and amounts paid or to be paid to the carrier.

Today, in the transportation industry, many tools exist to assist a freight company, broker, agent, and drivers to keep track of the business. In the business of freight broker and agent for the transportation industry, equipment and technology go together hand in hand.

You may need:

- A computer in your office and being computer literate helps. Your computer should be equipped with Internet service and you may find it necessary to produce memos, letters, financial invoices, reports and many others.
- A multiline-capable telephone is ideal. You may want to forward the line to another number such as an answering service or a cellular phone.
- Fax machine or a fax capability on a computer or a .pdf file in lieu of a fax.

- Additional software i.e. dispatch software can help if you plan to dispatch multiple loads per day.
- Carrier files retain a list of the qualifications applied to each carrier file. Files should always be complete. You may need to review it quickly every time a load is hauled.
- Shipper files should remain complete and updated with new contact information. Review frequently and modify information so that your office can better serve the client.

Other necessary office equipment may include a copier, file cabinets, a cellular phone, office space and location. Joining various industry groups and local traffic club can be informative and helpful. This will allow you to exchange information, contacts and ideas.

As you and your business continues to grow, you may want to include financial files composed of a general ledger, income statement or profit and lost statement, balance sheet, daily financial checklist, checkbook register, bank reconciliation, bill of lading, and 1099s.

For success in this business and in any business - time management is a must. Save time and use it to your benefit. The more time you save, the more you can accomplish. If it takes you three hours a week to balance your check book and write out your accounts payable checks, that may be several loads fewer than you have the opportunity to move freight. That could mean several hundred dollars less each month, or several thousands of dollars per year.

You may choose to outsource some of the functions that are an integral part of your weakness or those that you find tedious.

Knowledge Does Not Replace Experience.

It is generally agreed that experience is based on practice and practice makes perfect. While practice may not always make perfect, it is necessary to make certain you recognize the value of experience in business. The people who specialize in specific types of services are experienced at their craft which is gained largely through practice. The term experience implies that a person has had many more experiences in a particular area than the typical person. You can always benefit from those who are more experienced and are willing to share their knowledge. This alone is reason enough to join various trade industry organizations and attend their meetings.

You can always learn something from someone who has had more or different experiences than you. If you choose not to listen and learn, then you may find yourself troubleshooting the same problem they have already solved. You can waste your time 'reinventing the wheel' or learn from your experienced partners' past experiences. Instead of reinventing the wheel, you should be making new and improved wheels that go twice as fast.

Experiences

The benefit of experience obtained by someone else can teach you many things that can save you liability headaches, regulatory problems, and many other issues. Until you can run a brokerage with only a pencil and paper, until you can quote rates and lanes in 45seconds off the top of your head because you know where the trucks are, you have moved so much freight for so long that you are an expert, you should use every resource possible. Once you are that proficient and familiar with the marketplace, you will be successful.

Your knowledge has become experience when you really understand freight flows and lanes. When you have you have the practical working knowledge of the supply and demand in most major metropolitan cities. When you can locate a city, town, or suburb on a map in a few seconds, when you have created accustom-tabbed or electronic Rolodex which contains contacts of every shipper, broker, and half the carriers throughout the United States you're experienced.

Acquiring knowledge is step one. You are attaining the knowledge. In order for the knowledge to help you become successful, you must use it. Learn everything you can about the industry you are operating in, and since it changes daily, realize this is not a one-time research project.

Chapter 6: Familiarize Yourself with Industry Terms

Every business has its own jargon or language and the logistic trade is no different. Here are common terms in the freight and transportation industry that you will want to become familiar with. You don't have to learn them all at once, just keep your booklet handy to serve as a guide.

As a broker, you must be aware of all modes of transporting freight. Included are terms for air, cargo railroad, and LTI freight. When negotiating for air, cargo railroad, and LTI freight these terms will serve useful.

Different brokers develop specific areas of expertise. A word to the wise - learn as much as you can about the area of brokerage for the company for which you work.

If a broker is dealing with a mode of transportation with which it is not familiar for example a trucking broker is asked by a shipper to expedite freight by way of air carriage, you have to refer the shipper to a freight broker who has experience for that particular mode of transportation.

It will be expected that you are able to communicate with a working knowledge and intelligently when contacted by a potential customer, even when referring the client to another freight broker.

International Commercial Terms (INCOTERMS) define the duties of the buyer and the seller at each step in the movement of international goods.

Here's a Summary of INCOTERMS

Ex Works (EXW)- The seller makes the goods available at their docks. The buyer is responsible for all costs and risks involved in taking the goods from the seller's dock to the destination. This INCOTRTM provides minimum risk for the seller.

Free Carrier (FCA) – The seller fulfills their duties when the goods, cleared for export, are given to the carrier chosen by the buyer at a name place. The buyer assumes risk at the point of exchange and pays for all freight.

Free Alongside Ship (FAS) – The seller's obligation is to deliver the goods alongside the ship on the quay. The buyer then assumes all risks and costs from that point. The buyer must also provide export clearance.

Free on Board (FOB) – The seller delivers the goods to the ship and has fulfilled their duty when the goods pass over the ship's rail at the named port. This means that the seller pays for loading charges, pays for loading charges, pays freight charges to the named port and provides export clearance. The buyer bears all costs and risks from that point on.

Carriage Paid To (CPT) – The seller pays the freight costs to the named destination as well as provides export clearance. Once the goods have been delivered to the carrier, risk is transferred to the buyer.

Carriage and Insurance Paid To (CIP) purchase cargo insurance in the name of the buyer while the goods are in transit to the named port of shipment. The seller must also pay loading costs, unloading costs if they are included in the freight, and provide export clearance.

Cost and Freight (CFR) – The seller arranges and pays for transportation to the named port of destination, but risk and any other costs while on the ship are passed to the buyer as the goods pass over the ship's rail at port of shipment. The seller must also pay loading costs, unloading costs if they are included in the freight, and provide export clearance.

Cost, Insurance, and Freight (CIF) – The seller not only has the identical obligations as in CFR but must provide marine insurance while the goods are in transit in the name of the buyer. The buyer may wish to purchase additional insurance the seller must provide only minimum coverage. At the port of destination, the buyer pays all unloading costs if they are already included in the freight and assumes all risks and costs from the port of destination.

Delivered at Frontier (DAF) – The seller fulfills his or her risk and costs duties when the goods are made available, cleared for export at the named point and placed at the frontier, but prior to the customs border of the adjoining country. The buyer takes delivery at the named frontier.

Delivered Ex Ship(DES) – The seller meets his or her duties when the goods have been made available to the buyer on board the ship unclear for import at the named port of destination. All risk and costs involved in getting the goods to the named port of destination is the seller's. The buyer takes delivery at the port of destination, pays unloading fees, and provides import clearance.

Delivered Ex Quay (DEQ) – This means that he seller meets his or her
 obligations when the goods are made available to the buyer on the wharf (quay) at the named port of destination, cleared for importation. The seller assumes all risks and costs, including duties, taxes, and any other charges in delivering the goods. The buyer's obligation begins after taking delivery from the quay at port of destination.

Delivered Duty Unpaid (DDU) – The seller's duties end after the goods have been made available to the buyer at the named place in the country of importation. He or she has to pay the costs and assume the risks involved in bringing the goods to the named place of destination. The buyer pays the duties, taxes, and fees. The buyer simply takes delivery of the goods at the named place and costs and risks transfer here. This is the maximum obligation that can be assumed by the seller.

Intermodal Freight or "multimodal" – means any shipment using two or multiple modes of freight transportation during the transport process.

Door to door – the broker will arrange for the transportation from the shippers dock to the receiver's door.

Less-than-Truckload - loads that require less space than the standard 53' or 48' trailer and weigh less than 10,000 pounds a full truckload at a least expensive mode of transportation.

Full Truckload – utilizing the standard trailer of 53' or 48' at a maximum weight of up to 80,000 pounds gross vehicle weight to operate in the United States.

Shipper – any source that hires a carrier to transport goods to a receiver.

Distribution Center (DC) – usually a large retail store will purchase freight from a manufacturer requesting the shipment be delivered directly. The DC may serve as a receiver or consignee for many truck load deliveries.

A third-party logistics (3PL) supply-chain participant provides a broad range of services to its client.

 Just-In-Time (JIT) - some manufacturers ship raw materials and finished products that are time-sensitive with strict delivery guidelines that large fines are imposed upon for any delays. While JIT freight does bring a bonus of a higher price, if ineffective performances of any type, these types of shipments can be disastrous if inadequate contracts or carriers.

Types of Shippers

Refrigerated "reefer" or refrigerated trailers – self-contained refrigerator and freezer units and used to haul perishable items that must be transported at a certain temperature. Some refrigerated trailers can be used to haul dry freight but others cannot because of trailer sizes and door-opening limitations. Refrigerated trailers are heavier than dry van trailers because of the added weight of the refrigeration units, so they cannot handle as much cargo as a dry van trailer. Used frequently in the transport of grocery and produce items.

Flatbed – a floor, with straps and braces to hold freight. Usually the flatbed offers little or no protection from the elements. Used primarily for trees, lumber, and large construction parts.

Owner Operators- In addition to trucking companies, there are independents owneroperators who own and operate a truck or several trucks and have carrier authority.

Types of Freight & Cargo

There are many types of shippers and carriers. Freight falls under some general categories but specific types of freight and the requirements for carrying the freight is endless.

Freight of all Kinds (FAK) – FAK is the largest category of freight which includes many different types of freight to include consumer goods and manufactured products. A good rule of thumb is if the product can be found at a Walmart store, it is probably FAK freight.

Foodstuff – While foodstuff can also be found in the Walmart stores, it is entered in a separate category all its own. Foodstuff is any perishable item that can be stored in a cabinet or panty space and is hauled in a dry van trailer. Quality and spoilage of foodstuffs can be burden to the trucking company.

High-Dollar Cargo – Cargo deemed at a greater risk for theft and damages. A term adopted by the cargo insurance industry and used by many carriers usually covers freight being hauled up to a value of $100,000. Carriers have increased the value of coverage to $250,000 or up to $500,000. Most of the high-dollar commodities are commonly excluded from cargo insurance policies. Additional cargo insurance premiums are typically charged to obtain the additional insurance.

Hazardous Materials – (Haz-Mat) According to the U. S. Department of Transportation (DOT) defines hazardous waste material as a substance or material, including a hazardous substance, which has been determined by the Secretary of Transportation to be capable of posing an unreasonable risk to health, safety and property when transported in commerce, and which has so been designated.

Haz-Mat - Includes any product that may be shipped that because of its contents or properties can cause loss of life or damage to property or the environment if involved in an accident.Brokers involved with haz-mat transportation need to register with the DOT and meet training requirements. In order to haul hazardous materials, the carrier must be authorized by the FMCSA, under the DOT, and the driver must have a CDL license with a haz-mat endorsement.

Should a load of hazardous maters be involved in an accident, regardless of the seriousness of the accident or the class of the haz-mat product, and approved environmental cleanup group must be at the scene to assist in the de-containment and cleanup process. The cleanup process is expensive and payment for services is the responsibility of whoever is at fault unless otherwise agreed upon in the carriage contract.

If the loss is due to an accident, the cost is usually the responsibility of the carrier. If the loss is due to improper packaging or loading, the cost could be the responsibility of the shipper.

There are other factors that may cause a trucking company to decide to find hazardous materials the too costly to handle. Other reasons will be discussed in the class on logistic training.

Bill of Lading – a transportation document that is the contract of carriage between the shipper and carrier. It provides a receipt for the goods the shipper tenders to the carrier and may show certificate of title.

Broker – an intermediary between the shipper and the carrier. The broker arranges transportation for shippers and secures carriers to provide the actual truck transportation. A broker does not assume responsibility for the cargo and usually does not take possession of the cargo.

Common Carrier – A for-hire carrier that holds itself out to serve the general public at reasonable rates and without discrimination to operate, the carrier must secure a certificate of public convenience and necessity.
 Connecting Carrier – a carrier that interchanges trailers with another transportation line

Dispatching – The carrier activities involved with controlling equipment, involves arranging for fuel, drivers, crews, equipment and terminal space.

Freight – any commodity being transported

Lumper – a person who assists a motor carrier driver in the loading and unloading of property and commonly used in the food industry.

Hope you learned a lot. Remember you don't have to learn everything all at once. Keep your guidebook handy. Learn as you go.

Chapter 7: Build the Steps to Become a Broker

This is a booming industry . . .

Although no numbers exist for this market, experts predict that the industry will continue to grow.

As a Freight Broker

We are prepared to offer talented, ambitious people with the opportunity to become top brokers in the business and to take your career to the next level.

As a freight broker you will earn substantial commissions and be in control as an independent contractor in control of your own business.

High energy and sales results that will inspire and motivate you to meet your goals as a freight broker and provide exceptional service to our clients.

 If you are ready to make a positive and new transition of your broker agent career, you must be able to

Thrive in an environment where earnings potential is dictated by performance

- Have a strong background in business-to business outbound calling and sales A positive, motivated can-do attitude

- Must be aggressive, organized and effective under pressure
- Competitive energy to excel beyond goal expectations and a desire to win
- Strong negotiating and problem-solving skills
- Excellent written and verbal communication skills
- Ability to work independently
- A proven sales background documented success and not afraid of monthly numbers
- Demonstrated excellent time management, organizational and multitasking skills
- Customer service approach with a sense of urgency
- Unwavering integrity
- Have a home computer, high speed internet, home phone & fax

You Must Be Committed to:

- Participate in efforts to grow the brokerage business and increase the market presence of your logistic company to be a premier freight broker and logistics provider
- Build a solid client base of shippers and carriers. You will be in daily contact with building relationships, solving problems, and assessing the clients who need to meet along with company's goals
- Ready to work immediately
- Establish relationships with carriers and shippers

- Solicit new shipper businesses
- Solicit new carrier businesses
- Conduct freight bidding and quoting
- Manage customer relationships
- Coordinates with administration to ensure that accounts are current
- Prepare and coordinate required reporting documentation
- Proactively manage exceptions and provide solutions between shippers and carriers
- Communicate information timely and accurately

Broker

Another task you will need to accomplish is setting your office policies. The more thought you give to it early on, while your business is small, the better you will be able to handle growth later. Make sure you decide on official policies for issues like business hours, customer service policies and procedures, housekeeping rules, security, incident reporting, documentation systems, management policies, new client welcome program and many more.

General Operations

Keeping your office running smoothly requires you to complete many different tasks simultaneously. Either in between customers or after hours, you'll be organizing your notes, files and other pertinent information, cleaning, straightening and replenishing paper supply items, ordering supplies, documenting receipts, bookkeeping, documenting time spent, checking on the drivers, answering the telephone, and a whole host of other tasks, many of which are noticeable only if they do not get done.

Maximizing Cash Flow

There are several ways to make sure you have enough money available for running your business. Most of them involve vigilance. Try these strategies:

- Watch your expenditures
- Look for ways to save money
- Keep an eye on your accounts receivable
- Keep your overhead low
- Borrow ahead Put the money back into the business
- Be cautious
- Document, document, document
- Use a planner
- Keep well-ordered files
- Organize your information
- Write out detailed policies & procedures

Chapter 8: Consider the Big Picture

Other growing trends you may want to consider in the transportation freight and logistic business could include . . .

Excellent Customer Service

Even though you may not deal with customers face-to-face, you still need to give them good customer service. Here are a few aspects specific to business:

- Provide quick and timely service
- Respond promptly to queries
- Acknowledge orders
- Check for incomplete transactions
- Notify customers of timelines
- Stay connected with your clients (shippers and carriers)
- Cheerful attitude
- Personal approach
- Dedication
- Innovation

The most successful way to build a business is by recommendations. Studies show that although advertising in the Yellow Pages, on the Internet, and through the mail can result in a lot of inquires those do not reliably translate to sales. However, recommendations are much more effective.

Many entrepreneurs will tell you 'word of mouth' is the most important way to become known. Enlist the help of your friends and relatives to get the word out. Words quickly spread. Don't be afraid to ask them to help spread the word about your new business.

Often it doesn't take much. Word of mouth is the best kind of advertising. So make it work for you. Here are a few ideas you may want to use:

Customer testimonials: When you get a super satisfied customer or client who compliments the way you handle his business, ask if you can quote that person in your company's website or information. Most people will be happy to allow this.

Driver's praises: Maybe one of your drivers or associates is fascinated by the way you troubleshoots an unforeseen problem quickly and diligently. Ask if the praise can be included in your information. You will be surprised at the type of interest and business such praises can attract for your office.

Vendor or manufacturer endorsements: These can be put into your information as well especially if a vendor or manufacture company is well known.

Make Your Business Shine

- Provide excellent customer service
- Exceed expectations
- Guard your reputation
- Be reliable and resourceful

- Keep learning
- Stay well informed
- Join professional organizations
- Learn from others
- Look toward the future
- Evaluate your progress
- Have I carefully analyzed demand and adjusted to change?
- Have I kept good control of overhead cost and maximized my resources?
- Are my cash reserves sufficient?
- Does my company or office provide the kind of customer service that keeps clients coming back?
- Above all, remember why you got into the industry or into any business in the first place and what you want to accomplish in it!!!
- Be a good citizen, employee, and client.
- Deliver what you promise.
- Deal fairly with others.
- Enjoy what you do.
- Learn the skills you need to be a successful and profitable Freight Broker:
- Recognize the progression of freight brokering from start to finish.
- Have the tools needed to be successful and effective as a freight agent.
- Learn the essentials of day-to-day operations and tasks of a freight brokering as an agent.
- Use techniques and skills such as prospecting, sales, marketing, freight costs and negotiations.
- Be able to accomplish and manage a freight shipment from origin to destination.

- Gain valuable and knowledgeable freight industry resources and assets with us.

This is an ideal home-based career opportunity. This booklet serves as an overview and does not in any way represent the abridge publication containing all of the necessary information necessary for a successful career in the logistic business. It does, however, get you started.

What You Can Expect

Once you have your authority, and are operational, you can be reasonably certain that problems will arise. These problems can be grouped into the following categories: Mechanical, Regulatory, Financial, and Communication. I will briefly go into each category and give a short example of experiences that I have had with regard these problems.

Mechanical Problems

Your equipment WILL break down. Hopefully you will have some form of financing to pay for the repairs. Statistically, you have a very good chance of needing tire repair, but there are thousands of other things that CAN go wrong with your equipment.

Usually trailers do not give you many problems. Tires, brakes, wheel bearings, air lines, and lights are by far the most common repairs made to trailers. $1,500 will usually be enough to fix anything that can go wrong with a trailer.

Tractors have several different systems. Each of these systems can malfunction and most definitely will at some point in time. Tractors have fuel, electrical, lubrication, cooling, air, and exhaust systems. Special tools and skills are needed to perform repairs on any of these systems. If you have a background in heavy equipment repair and understand the systems in a truck and have the tools to fix these systems; you have an IMMENSE advantage in the trucking industry! We have spent about $10,000 on repairs for our truck and we have owned it for 26 months. We have had to get two tires fixed, front leaf springs replaced, one axle brake pads replaced, EGR Valve replaced, Turbocharger replaced, Clutch replaced, and some minor repairs too.

Regulatory Problems

Regulatory problems will arise at some point in time until you become accustomed to the schedule of when you have to file documents and pay fees. I wish there was a way to automate these things and have automatic drafts done on our account for payment, but there is not. We always need to actually fill out some forms, answer a few questions, or read some new information. It is a nuisance to deal with and it never stops. You spend your valuable time with this stuff.

Financial Problems

If you plan well and are responsible with your money, you should not have many financial problems. Insurance is classified as financial (fiduciary) and ALWAYS is a problem. Your insurance company may drown you in paperwork that you need to read and sign ALL THE TIME!

Communication Problems

No, I am not talking about phones or Internet connections here. I am talking about people, who are supposed to know what to do when you mail them paperwork or submit forms online, messing your stuff up. Then you have to backtrack and chase them down on the phone to straighten your stuff out. I find that many people will overcharge you a dollar or two for a service or product and make you sit on the phone for 45 minutes to recover your money. I strongly believe that this is intentional and not a "clerical error" as they tell me. Think about it, for every person who is willing to sit on the phone to recover what is rightfully theirs; how many are not willing to sit on the phone? These companies probably make millions of dollars on these small overcharges. Also, many times you will be given wrong pickup numbers or delivery numbers for your loads. Then you have to sit on the phone for MORE time to get the correct data. Also you will have accessorial charges (lumpers and detention are among accessorial charges) that you usually have to call someone about.

Basically communication problems are somebody trying to keep money that is rightfully yours (or messing something up that could infringe on your business) and you having to spend your valuable time correcting it. Instead of that valuable time going to expanding your business, you are spending that valuable time cleaning up a mess that someone else plops in your lap. Why people cannot just do something as you wish it to be done and not add their own "flavor"; I will never understand. Your time IS MONEY, and communication problems cost you time that you should be spending getting ahead instead of simply maintaining the status quo.

Chapter 9: What to Spend (Or Not Spend) Money On

One of the main problems you will encounter when you get your own authority is what to spend your money on and what not to spend your money on. I'm going to be honest with you in saying that I am pretty experienced with this, but not yet an expert. I will give you some of my experiences as well as some numbers to back up what I recommend. Remember that EVERYTHING you do in business is about profit (the bottom line).

Every decision in business (especially when you first start out) revolves around what your business's needs are at the time you are making the decision. Another thing about business decisions is that they are not static. In other words, just because you make a business decision TODAY about a particular problem DOES NOT mean that you will make the same decision two months from now when the same problem comes up. Two months from now, the financial standing of your business may be significantly different than it is today!

A very good example of this very phenomenon is factoring. Let's say that you decide to factor a load that paid $1800 today because you need money to pay fuel and your 2290. Then in two months from now you decide not to factor that same load that pays $1800 because you have plenty of money in your account to pay for fuel and you don't have to worry about your 2290. It's the same pay for the same load right? You made two different decisions with regard to the same paying load because your business situation was different than it was two months ago. You will run across this all the time in business. There will be times you want to wait for the most profit over time. There will be times where you will take less than the prevailing rate for a particular lane to achieve some other goal with regard to your customer or another customer. There will be times when you will absolutely rob someone with your rates because it is a very bad lane and you don't care if you ever haul for a particular customer again or haul in that lane again. (For me, that is NJ, NY, and New England. I don't care, you want us to go in there, you are paying BIG TIME or you can get someone else to go there)

So, let's get back to the subject matter of this chapter, what to spend money on. I generally have found it to be prudent to spend money on things that save me money over a long period of time. A great example of this is fuel efficient tires. We purchased eight brand new Yokohama TY 517 MC2 tires almost two years ago. They had a price of around $3200. We have all eight tires still (no blowouts) and they have gotten us around a half a mile per gallon fuel economy improvement over the previous tires. We have operated our truck for about 275,000 miles on those tires. The average fuel price over that period has been $3.40 so basically the tires have saved us $13,008.69 on fuel over that span. If you subtract the cost of the tires; that is close to $10,000 we were able to keep in our pockets. A fantastic investment indeed! And we still have at least a half inch of tread left on those tires, so the savings will keep coming! It was well worth it to spend our money on those tires when we did. That is the point I am trying to make with this chapter, there are good investments and bad ones.

With the foregoing said, I will share what I have found to be good investments and what are not good investments.

Good Investments

- Trade associations that offer quantity discount fuel pricing on their fuel cards and other services
- Oil Testing
- Scan Gauge D
- Fleet air filter
- Complete diagnostic
- Internet Truckstop (or similar online service)
- Alignment
- Bypass oil filtration system
- Low rolling resistance tires
- Fixing something that will malfunction BEFORE it malfunctions

Bad Investments

- Chrome
- Unneeded "Professional" services
- Excessive insurance
- MOST transactions where someone acts as your "agent"

Chapter 10: Discover Self Pace & Time Management Success

We've all heard the saying "time is money", and that phrase is essentially true. Unfortunately, time doesn't always equal money though. Time is continually passing but that doesn't mean you are continually making money, this depends on how you manage your time and what you do with it. Here are 9 reasons time management is important.

9 Reasons Why Time Management is Important

1. Time is limited - Everyone gets the same amount of time each day, and it's limited, therefore it's important to make the most of your time if you ever want to be more than average at the workplace.

2. Accomplish more with less effort - By taking control of your time, you're able to stay focused on the task at hand. This leads to higher efficiency since you never lose momentum. Imagine running a mile where you stop every 5 seconds, this would cause you to become exhausted very quickly and take much longer to complete the run.

3. Make better decisions - There are many choices in life and often-times we're faced with many choices to choose from at the same time. When you practice good time management, you have more

time to breathe; this allows you to determine which choices are the best to make.When you feel pressed for time and have to make a decision, you're more likely to jump to conclusions and not fully consider the different options; this leads to poor decision making.

4. Be more successful - Time management is the key to success; it allows you to take control of your life rather than follow the flow of others. You accomplish more, you make better decisions, and you work more efficiently; this leads to a more successful life.

5. Learn more - When you control your time and work more efficiently, you're able to learn more and increase your experience faster. There's a reason some students graduate earlier than others, so imagine implementing time management throughout your entire career. You'll not only stand out from the rest, but you'll gain experience must faster and be able to move up in life a lot sooner.

6. Reduce stress - One of the main causes of stress is due to people feeling rushed. The phrase "I have so much to do and so little time to do it" is generally spoken with frustration which leads to stress. With good time management, you know how much time you have, how long it will take to get your tasks done, you accomplish more, and have more free time. This gives you more breathing room, which reduces the feeling of being rushed, which in turn leads to less frustration and stress.

7. Higher quality work - We all need some free time to relax and unwind but, unfortunately, many of us don't get much free time because we're too busy trying to keep up with our daily activities and work load. By implementing time management skills, you are able to get more done in a shorter period of time leading to more free time.

8. Creates discipline - When you practice good time management in your life, you are less likely to procrastinate. Time management leads to higher productivity and leads to a disciplined life.

About the Expert

Bruce Stimson started his factoring career in 2001, when he founded QLFS, which eventually became the Invoice Trucking Group. Mr. Stimson led the firm through its initial growth and established it as a leading provider to startups and small companies in the New England region.

After QLFS, Mr. Stimson launched Trucking Capital LLC to provide services in the USA, Canada and Australia. Under his leadership, Trucking Capital LLC has expanded to offer a number of business finance products and can help companies in most industries.

Trucking Capital LLC is one of the few companies that offers micro-factoring (also called small-ticket factoring), which helps early-stage companies with limited revenues. Small business factoring has been ignored by larger factoring firms and banks, establishing Mr. Terry as a pioneer in this market.

Before starting his career in finance, Mr. Stimson held several management positions in operations and marketing in the telecommunications industry for eight years. He earned a Master's Degree in Finance with a concentration in banking.

HowExpert publishes quick 'how to' guides on all topics from A to Z by everyday experts. Visit HowExpert.com to learn more.

Recommended Resources

- <u>HowExpert.com</u> – Quick 'How To' Guides on All Topics from A to Z by Everyday Experts.
- <u>HowExpert.com/free</u> – Free HowExpert Email Newsletter.
- <u>HowExpert.com/books</u> – HowExpert Books
- <u>HowExpert.com/courses</u> – HowExpert Courses
- <u>HowExpert.com/clothing</u> – HowExpert Clothing
- <u>HowExpert.com/membership</u> – HowExpert Membership Site
- <u>HowExpert.com/affiliates</u> – HowExpert Affiliate Program
- <u>HowExpert.com/writers</u> – Write About Your #1 Passion/Knowledge/Expertise & Become a HowExpert Author.
- <u>HowExpert.com/resources</u> – Additional HowExpert Recommended Resources
- <u>YouTube.com/HowExpert</u> – Subscribe to HowExpert YouTube.
- <u>Instagram.com/HowExpert</u> – Follow HowExpert on Instagram.
- <u>Facebook.com/HowExpert</u> – Follow HowExpert on Facebook.